WE FOUND THEM

ANTHONY ESPADA

Archway Publishing books may be ordered through booksellers or by contacting:

Archway Publishing
1663 Liberty Drive
Bloomington, IN 47403
www.archwaypublishing.com
844-669-3957

ISBN: 978-1-6657-0149-5 (sc)
ISBN: 978-1-6657-0150-1 (e)

Library of Congress Control Number: 2021900603

Print information available on the last page.

Archway Publishing rev. date: 01/26/2021

CLEVELAND, OHIO

MAY 6, 2013

WE HAD JUST FINISHED ROLL CALL AT THE CLEVELAND Division of Police Second District Police Station. It was approximately fifteen hundred hours, or three in the afternoon civilian time. It was a beautiful Monday afternoon. The sun was out, and the temperature was in the low seventies. My partner that day was Officer Michael Tracy. We had just completed our vehicle check and were headed out on patrol. Mike was driving that day. I was the passenger and what was called the writer—the one who writes, operates the car radio, and handles pretty much all contact with citizens who call for service. All necessary reports are completed by the writer as well.

Then the following day we would switch off: Mike would write, and I would drive. This gave each officer a break in routine every other day. Our call sign that day was 2A23 (2 Adam 23). Our first assignment that day was an alarm drop. We responded to the location and checked the residence. It checked OK at the time. All doors and windows were secure. False Alarm.

After giving dispatch our disposition of the alarm, we received another assignment to respond to a department store. Security was holding a couple of shoplifters. Upon our arrival at the department store and conferring with security, they decided not to prosecute. Protocol prior to releasing these individuals was to check and make sure they did not have any active warrants before we released them. They did not, per our dispatch, so they were warned and released.

For the next hour or so, all was quiet. We pretty much gave

our assigned area (zone) special attention. We drove around the up-and-coming Tremont area neighborhood, and everyone was out enjoying the beautiful day. At approximately 1650 hours (4:50 p.m.), we pulled up to a disabled vehicle off to the side of the road. For safety reasons we stayed and assisted the driver until his private tow arrived. After we assisted the driver with his tow, we began giving our zone special attention once again.

We decided to give the area of the West Side Market attention. The West Side Market is Cleveland's oldest publicly owned market. It opened its doors in 1912. We continued to patrol the area and observed nothing unusual, just everyone out enjoying the great weather we were having.

Within the next few minutes, my life would change forever. All eyes from around the world would be focused on what was about to happen.

At 1752 hours (5:52 p.m.), the car radio came to life. Dispatch: "2 Adam 23 for a Code 1." A Code 1 is the highest priority assignment you can receive. It means *stop what you are doing and head to that location fast.* I picked up the radio mic and acknowledged dispatch.

Me: "2 Adam 23, go ahead."

Dispatch: "2 Adam 23, can you head to 2210 Seymour Avenue? There is a female on the line calling and stating she is Amanda Berry, and she has been kidnapped for ten years and is requesting help."

Mike and I immediately looked at each other. We could not believe what we had just heard.

Me: "Is she still on the line?"

Dispatch: "Yes, she is saying she has been kidnapped for ten years. She says she is safe now. She is also mentioning an Ariel Castro, who might be the suspect who took her."

The West Side Market was not far from Seymour Avenue. Mike immediately turned on the lights and sirens and started heading toward Seymour Avenue. In the past years since Amanda Berry had been missing, numerous crank calls would come in saying they had information on Amanda.

Just the previous year, in July 2012, the FBI had received a tip from an inmate from Lucasville prison claiming he had killed Amanda Berry and buried her body in a field. They dug up the whole corner of an empty lot. Nothing was found. That corner was less than a mile from Seymour Avenue, our destination. I looked at Mike and said, "If this is another fake call, we are going to find who called this in, and they are going to jail!" We then turned on to Seymour Avenue, and we could see a small crowd ahead of us. They were all on Mike's side of the car, the driver's side, as we were pulling up. I could see a young female holding a child, standing there on the sidewalk. I looked at Mike, and I asked him, "Is it her?" Mike could not tell, because we were not close enough yet. As soon as Mike stopped the car, I asked again, "Is it her?"

She walked up to Mike's side window, and at that moment, Mike looked at me and said, "It's her."

NEW YORK

MARCH 6, 1970

I was born in the borough of Manhattan in New York City, well known as Spanish Harlem. We were a poor Puerto Rican family. It was just my mom and my two brothers for a while. I never met my biological father or even saw a picture of him. My stepfather came into the picture when I was about two years old. He has been with us ever since. My stepfather stepped in and raised my two brothers and me. I always considered him my father and very much appreciate all he has done for us.

We lived in the borough of Queens as well, mostly until I was ten years old. My oldest brother was ten years older than I was, and my middle brother was seven years older than me. Living in New York City in the seventies was not the greatest. Lots of crime going on throughout the whole city. It was not a place to raise a family. At the age of six, in 1976, I had a traumatic incident that happened to me. I buried it away for years—until it was triggered on May 6, 2013, on Seymour Avenue, some thirty-seven years later.

I remember, as a kid, watching John Wayne war movies with my dad. I always told him, "I am going to be a marine one day!" He always encouraged me to do so. As the years went by, I got to experience major events in history. The major blackout in 1977 in New York City. I remember we did not leave the apartment for days due to all the violence and looting. Another big major event was the Son of Sam killings (the .44 Caliber Killer). He had the whole city walking on eggshells. It was a very scary time for every New Yorker. Let us not forget the 1977 World Series champions, the New York Yankees. That is when Reggie Jackson hit three home runs in game six to clinch the title. The most major event of all was the premiere of *Star Wars* in May 1977. I remember going to see it on a school field trip. How awesome was that!

Crime was getting bad. I remember we used to visit Cleveland, Ohio, every so often to see family we had there, kind of as a break and to get away from New York City. At the time, Cleveland was "country" for me. Very boring. One day, my mom and dad decided to move to Cleveland, Ohio. Their reason for moving to Ohio was me. They did not want me to grow up in an atmosphere where I could possibly end up in jail, on drugs, or dead. In the summer of 1980, we packed up my dad's Chevy Suburban with all the necessary items, and we drove west to Cleveland, Ohio.

I hated it! I did not want to move. All my family was back in New York—grandparents, aunts, uncles, cousins, and friends. I was ten years old at the time. I went from a big city that never sleeps to the country, where nothing was going on. My mom and my dad tried to make me understand their reasoning for the move, but I just would not get it. The drive from New York to Cleveland was about eight hours long. I complained the whole time. I am sure my parents were already fed up with me.

We arrived at nighttime at my stepfather's sister's house. I was so tired. I just wanted to go to bed. So, after we got settled in, I went to bed while everybody else stayed up eating and catching up. The next morning, I woke up and went outside to see the neighborhood we were in. All I saw was a bunch of houses, big yards, lots of trees, and grass. I came from living in an apartment building in Queens—no backyards, no grass, and trees were mostly in the city parks. All I thought was, *I am in the country for sure! This sucks!*

It was quiet, too quiet. I wanted to go back home. The crazy thing was not knowing then that on the street where we lived, I would meet my high school sweetheart and future wife, who lived about six houses down from us. That would not happen until a few years from then. After a few months living there, we moved a few miles away. Mom enrolled me in school, where I began the fifth grade.

I started meeting new friends, but I still was homesick. My mom and I finally came to a compromise. I guess she got tired of all my complaining. She decided that every summer break, she would send me back to New York for the summer with my grandparents. I got to see all my friends and family for a couple of months. It was great! The summers came and went, and I would head back home before school started. This went on for three or four years.

Then I started meeting new friends. I was getting used to Cleveland. My visits to New York would become less and less, until the summer visits just stopped. I started spending my summers here in Cleveland instead. Cleveland was not so bad after all.

A friend of mine from school was having a birthday party one evening. She lived on the street where we first moved to Cleveland. I remember my mom was not going to let me go, but my dad convinced her that it would be OK. My friend, Mike, came to pick me up to go to the party. We walked to the party together. I probably was about fourteen years old at the time. We arrived at the party, and all our friends were there listening to music and dancing. My buddy Mike knew most of the people there and was introducing me to some. Mike, who was one year ahead of me, introduced me to one of his class-mates, Sandra, who happened to have a sister there with her, Vivian. After meeting both, I remember the exact dress Vivian was wearing. White dress with blue polka dots all over it. I was able to get my courage up and ask her to dance. She said *yes!* We pretty much talked and danced most of the evening and had a great time. It started getting late, so I had to leave. Mike decided he would leave also. We all said bye to everyone and started the walk back home. I remember till this day that on that walk home, I looked at Mike and told him, "I really like that girl I was talking to and dancing with."

He then told me, "Next time you see her, ask her out." I told him that I had forgotten her name. He then said, "I think her name is Evelyn." Yeah, that sounded right, Evelyn.

I remember telling him, "Mike, I think she is the one. I like her a lot, and I think she is really the one"—not knowing how right I was that evening.

It took about a day or two before I was able to get her phone number. I would call and ask for her sister Sandra, since she was older, and Sandra would put her on the phone to talk. It was bothering me, and I had to ask her, "Your name is Evelyn, right?"

She yelled into the phone, "*No*, it is Vivian!" I put the blame all on Mike, and we laughed it off. It was in about eighth or ninth grade that we began to date. I was a year ahead of her, so she probably was in eighth grade at the time. Wow, thinking back now, I realize we were kids, not knowing anything about anything. I knew in my heart, though, that she was the one.

We dated through junior high and high school. Her dad was extremely strict, and no dating was allowed. So, when I used to walk her home from school, I would drop her off a block or two from her house so as to not get caught by her dad. This went on for over a year or so. Then one day, not sure what happened, but I was able to walk her all the way home and leave her at the front gate. I was not allowed beyond the front gate, though. As time went on, I was then allowed to visit her, but only to stand by the front gate. She would be on the inside part, and I would be on the outside part of the gate. We would stand there for hours talking. It just felt good being with her. We must have been dating for a couple of years by then.

Then one day while we were talking by the gate, her parents

were arriving home from grocery shopping. I would still get nervous seeing her dad. As they were starting to unload the car, her dad looked at me and said, "Are you just going to stand there or help us unload the groceries?" I was in shock! I did not know what to say, so I just started grabbing bags and followed him back toward their side door. That would be the first time I would be allowed in the house, and I dropped the grocery bags onto the kitchen floor. From that day forward, when I would come visit Vivian, I would be allowed in the house! We had to be around sixteen and seventeen years old by this time.

In high school, I worked at a fast-food restaurant, and Vivian worked at an ice cream shop just down the street. We were still dating strong, with some problems along the way, but we were able to work through them. Remember, we were still kids not knowing anything about anything.

Vivian knew I had always wanted to be a marine. I remember seeing the marine recruiters at the school talking to all the seniors. I could not wait to be a senior. I wanted in so badly. I wanted to be one of the few and the proud! Then the moment arrived: senior year! I was on the hunt looking for the chance to get to talk to a recruiter. I think a few months went by, and I did not see one recruiter during that time. The past couple of years, they had been everywhere, and now it was like, where did they all go? I do not recall the day in November 1987 when I asked my teacher if I could use the restroom. I got my hall pass and started walking down the hallway toward the restroom. Moments later, I happened to look up, and at the other end of the hallway, there was a marine in his dress blues walking toward me. *Holy shit! This is it!* I walked up to him and asked, "Sir, are you here recruiting?"

He immediately said, "Yes, are you interested?"

Without skipping a beat, I told him, "Where do I sign?" He was a staff sergeant. Looking so awesome in his uniform. Standing there in his dress blues, staring down at me. Locked and cocked. Creases in his uniform, so sharp they would probably cut you. About a week later, that staff sergeant was in my living room meeting my parents. I was seventeen years old at the time, so my parents had to sign papers for me to enter the delayed entry program. I passed the ASVAB test, which is required to enter any military branch. Now it was time to focus on my schoolwork and graduate from high school.

I had been dating Vivian now for about three or four years. School was going great, and I was on track to graduate in June. Vivian still had one more year to go, being a junior. Our relationship had evolved, and we tried to spend every moment with each other, as much as we could. It was around May, and Vivian had become sick and was always nauseated. Her mom had made an appointment at the doctor's office to see what the matter was with her being sick all the time. I remember going with her to her appointment. I waited and did not know what to expect, but in the back of my mind, I had a pretty good idea of what it could possibly be. Oh boy!

Some time went by, and Vivian came out of the doctor's office, looked at me, paused for a second, and said that she was pregnant. *I knew it.* I was happy and terrified at the same time. I do not know if we hugged, cried, or what. All we thought was, how were we going to tell her parents? Especially her dad, being as strict as he was. He was going to be furious! I was thinking, *I am dead.*

After the initial appointment, we told her mom she had the stomach flu or something. We waited a week before we said anything. Man, were we nervous as heck when the day finally came for us to tell her parents. We decided to tell her dad first. Might as well get the worst part out of the way. We both went up to Vivian's dad's bedroom, where he was watching TV. He knew I was joining the Marine Corps after high school graduation and knew I wanted to marry Vivian one day—not knowing that day would come sooner than we thought. We reminded him of my intentions toward his daughter, and then we told him. He sat up in his bed and just looked at us both and said, "What is done is done, and we cannot change it." He also wanted to make sure I would honor my intentions and do what I had said I was going to do. I could not believe it! I really thought he was going to react way differently, and I thought I was going to be sent to the hospital that day.

One down, one to go. He accompanied us outside to where Vivian's mom was doing yard work. Vivian's dad actually spoke for the both of us. He told her that Vivian was pregnant, and I planned to marry her after graduation from Marine Corps boot camp. Vivian's mom took it the hardest. She just stood there listening. She would not even look at us. I know her dad was trying to calm her down by talking to her, but yeah, she took the news hard. Vivian told me her mom did not talk to her for a while. Her mom also believed that when I went into the Marine Corps, I was not coming back for Vivian and the baby. I might have stayed away from their house for a while until things cooled down. Vivian would come over to my house to visit more at the time. My parents took the news much better but made sure I was sticking to my intentions on marrying Vivian.

It was getting close to graduation day, June 16, 1988. I would be the first in my family to graduate from high school. I was excited, and I believe my family was proud of me and my accomplishment. Vivian around this time was around three months pregnant. Her mom had calmed down quite a bit by this time, but she was still worried that I would leave and never come back for Vivian and the baby after boot camp. Graduation day came. It was a very proud moment for the whole family. Thinking back now, I saw that the sacrifice my mom and dad had made to get me away from New York City was worth it. They had given up a lot for me, so I had to return the favor by staying out of trouble and graduating from high school. I did it!

June 16 was on Thursday. That following Monday, June 20,

I would be standing on the yellow footprints in Parris Island, South Carolina, Marine Corps Boot Camp. I made the best of my last weekend at home by spending it mostly with Vivian. I was going to miss her so much.

That morning of June 20, Staff Sergeant picked me up around 6:00 a.m. to take me to the MEPS station to finish any last-minute paperwork and do my final swearing in. My family would meet me at the airport to say bye. My adrenaline was pumping. I could not believe I was going. I was going to be one of the few and the proud! From the MEPS station, they grouped us together in small groups. They did it by branch of service. Our group had about six to seven guys going into the Marine Corps. They gave us our orders and put us on the train to the airport for our flight.

After we got to the airport and checked in for our flight, the families of the other guys started showing up to say bye one last time. I just sat there waiting for mine to show up. I wanted to see my family one more time. It was going to be a long three to four months that I would be gone. Nobody was there yet. Then they started the boarding process onto the plane. I waited as long as I could, but no one showed up. So, I got on the plane. This was 1988, when everyone was allowed to the gate. I was later told that my family did show up right after they closed the doors to the plane. My mother told me she cried and pleaded with them to let her go in to say bye to me, but they would not let her. My mom said the plane was pulling away from the gate by then.

Vivian was not at the airport. We had said our goodbyes back at home. Plus, she was three months pregnant and occasionally would still get sick, so she was not feeling well that day. I told her I loved her and that I would be back to marry her after boot camp. Her mom still had her doubts, and if I am not mistaken, so did Vivian. Again, I knew in my heart she was the one and I was going to marry her.

JUNE 20, 1988

(NIGHTTIME)

After arriving in Savannah, Georgia, we had to take a bus ride to Parris Island, South Carolina. It was approximately a one-and-a-half-hour drive to get there from the airport. The bus was full from front to back, and every seat was taken by recruits from all walks of life. We did not know what to expect when we got there.

I remember pulling up to the receiving barracks at Parris Island. It was dark and late, and I was tired. It had to be close to midnight, and then I saw him. He was a staff sergeant, lean and really mean-looking. The bus's doors opened, and he walked up the steps and just stood there in the middle aisle, with uniform creases that looked razor-sharp and the traditional campaign cover, or "Smokey." Then he spoke—well, it was more like yelling: "You will all get off this bus and stand on my yellow footprints you see outside on the ground! You have thirty seconds! Now move!" He stood there in the aisle and did not move out of the way. We had to jump over each other and each seat in order to get off the bus, not daring to touch him either as we exited the bus climbing over each other. As we all made it out to the yellow footprints, we were all tired and were trying to stand there in some type of order or formation. I knew it was going to be a long night.

The games had just begun. From here on out, it was constant yelling, and I was thinking to myself, *What did I get myself into?* We spent a couple of hours filling out paperwork and getting our heads shaved. We also got our uniforms issued to us. It was a constant *go, go, go* for the next few hours. We finally got to bed around three or four in the morning. I was beat!

It seemed I had just closed my eyes when the lights came back on around 5:30 a.m. and the yelling started all over again. From this point on, I knew it was going to be a long four months. *Shit, what did I do?*

Boot camp went in three phases. Each phase was three to four weeks long, depending on the phase. The first phase was a transition phase from civilian life to recruit. A lot of physical training, first aid, and classes on Marine Corps history and drill. The second phase was learning about marksmanship skills, close-quarter combat skills, gas chamber training (that sucked), and rifle qualifications. The third phase was BWT (Basic Warrior Training). We learned survival skills and had field training exercises out in the woods, rain or shine. The third phase for me was toward the end of August, and graduation was September 15, 1988.

After BWT, we headed back to our barracks. By this time, we were one of the senior platoons in the battalion. Graduation day was a couple of weeks away. By now, we were pretty much getting fitted for our uniforms for graduation, as well as doing any last-minute paperwork, having medical appointments, and testing. Actual training was pretty much done. Just winding down toward graduation day.

During the last three to four months was the hardest

challenge I ever had to face. Just imagine every minute of your day was planned doing something. There was no downtime. Could not make phone calls home to your family. Just letters. Trust me, I wrote home every day complaining! But I stuck through it. They broke us all down from civilian life and built us back up to their standards, Marine Corps standards. I would do it all over again.

The day finally arrived! I had never felt so proud in my life. I had accomplished what only a few would dare to do. My dream had come true. I was a United States Marine! My family could not make it to the graduation ceremony, but that was OK. I knew they would be waiting for me at home and proud. After the graduation ceremony and all the congrats and hugs, things still moved pretty quickly. The marines whose families did not show up had to hurry back to the barracks to grab our gear and load onto the bus that was taking us to the airport. We had all earned ten days of leave at home before reporting to our school assignments. Man, we needed it! We all loaded the bus and were off to the airport.

I got back to Cleveland early in the afternoon that day. My brother picked me up from the airport. After the airport, we decided to go to our mom's work and surprise her. It had been four months since I had seen her. I was still in uniform, and I remember getting there and one of her coworkers going to get her. I stood off to the side so she could not see me. My mom walked out and saw my brother first. Then she turned and saw me standing there. Her youngest son, her baby, standing there tall and proud, a marine! She immediately ran into my arms crying and was so happy to see me. She held me there for a few minutes, not wanting to let me go. She was happy I was home and safe.

After she had showed me off to all her coworkers, I was able to finally go home and change. I could not wait to see Vivian. By now, she would be about six months pregnant. I finally got to see Vivian and her baby bump. She was beautiful as ever, and I had missed her so much. I saw the rest of the family, and they all congratulated me. It felt so good. Now I had to show them I was going to keep my promise.

I only had ten days to be home, so we started the process of getting our marriage license. Vivian's parents had to sign papers because she was seventeen years old at the time. Then we went to a small jewelry shop in downtown Cleveland and were able to get a set of wedding rings at a price I could afford. We had our license and our wedding rings, and so on September 23, 1988, we got married by a judge in court. My brother was a witness, and Vivian's sister was the other witness. After about fifteen to twenty minutes or so, we were husband and wife. I knew without a doubt Vivian was going to be the one from the first time I met her. Now here we were, married and about to have a baby in a few months.

After the small ceremony, we had a party at Vivian's parents' house with family and friends. I tried to have fun, but all I had in my mind was that I had to leave in a couple of days. This time it would be harder, because now I had a wife, a family of my own that I had to leave behind. Vivian wanted to come, but she could not. She still had one more year of school left. There was no way I was not going to let her finish school. Her parents would kill me!

Approximately September 25, 1988, I had to fly to California to start my school and training as an assault amphibian vehicle crewman. California was beautiful. The weather, the scenery, everything was beautiful. Totally different world out there. I would call Vivian twice a week to check in, see how things were back home, and update her on my progress in training. I would send money home for whatever she needed. I felt I still had a lot to prove to her mom, to show that I was not going anywhere. I know she still had her doubts and probably thought I was not coming back for Vivian, even though she was pregnant and we were married. My schooling and training lasted about three months, and in early December would be graduation from AAV school.

December 9, 1988 was graduation day, and I was able to go home for another ten days of leave. It all worked out perfectly because I graduated on the ninth of December. I got home on the tenth, Vivian went into labor on the eleventh, and our son Anthony Jr. was born on the twelfth. I was able to be home for the birth of my son! I cried like a baby. I could not believe I was a father. Another proud moment for me.

Time flew by so fast. My ten days of leave were coming to an end, and it felt like I only got to spend a short time with Vivian and our son. I hated leaving them behind again, but she still had to finish school. I knew the next six months were going to be difficult for Vivian, taking care of a newborn and going to school. Thanks to both our families for helping.

MARINE CORPS AIR GROUND COMBAT CENTER (MCAGCC)

TWENTYNINE PALMS, CALIFORNIA

I WAS STATIONED BACK IN CALIFORNIA, IN THE DESERT THIS time: Marine Corps Base in Twentynine Palms, California, located in the middle of the Mojave Desert. It is about forty to forty-five minutes outside of Palm Springs, California. What a culture shock for me. I mean besides the base, there was hardly anything out there at the time. Just outside of the base was the city of Twentynine Palms, with a population of eleven thousand. I was in the middle of nowhere.

I was assigned to Delta Company Third Assault Amphibian Battalion. At that time, I was living in the barracks with all the single marines. There was a six-month waiting list to get base housing for Vivian and me, so it should be timed perfectly for her to graduate from school and then we would be called for housing. Then I could send for her and the baby.

Meanwhile, I was pretty much getting accustomed to the rules and regulations of the unit, meeting new people from all around the country, and going through a lot of training. Being stationed in Twentynine Palms, we had approximately a thousand square miles of training ground that was all desert. As an AAV marine, you become responsible for operating and maintaining the vehicle and its weapon systems. AAVs are armored tracked vehicles that can transport up to twenty-five combat-loaded marines or up to ten thousand pounds of cargo in hostile land and in water operations. AAV platoons execute ship-to-shore operations and employ troops and weapons during ship-to-shore movements. An AAV weighted approximately twenty-six tons and cost over a million dollars, and here I was, nineteen years old and responsible for one!

Let us not forget about the weather out there in the Mojave Desert. Summertime, it can reach 115-120 degrees. Wintertime, it can get very cold. It can get to the low thirties, but by the afternoon it will warm up again. As time went by, I began to fall in love with the desert: the scenery, the mountains, cactus—everything about it. It was so peaceful.

I started to make good friends, from all backgrounds: rich, poor, country guys, and even guys from the big cities. The more we were together, the more we became a band of brothers.

Six months went pretty quickly, and by June 1989, Vivian would graduate from high school. Now I could send for her. I missed her and the baby so much. This would be the first time that I would see them since the baby was born. Anthony Jr. would be six months old by now. Base housing called and said our home was ready for move-in. It was perfect timing.

I called Vivian to let her know, and she started to prepare for their move out here. I had to make arrangements for our furniture and other belongings to be moved three thousand miles cross country. The great thing about this was that the military were the ones that moved your stuff. When moving day came, Vivian told me a semitruck pulled up to her parents' home and packed up all our belongings. One other thing about that day that Vivian had said was that she could tell that it was finally hitting her mom. Her mom was realizing that I was keeping my promise. She was very emotional that her daughter was leaving home, not just around the corner either. It would be three thousand miles away. About a week later, Vivian and Anthony Jr. would get on a plane and fly out to California. Finally, I would have my family with me!

They arrived at night, when I picked them up at the airport. They were both tired, but it was good to have them both with me. The next morning when Vivian looked out the window and there was nothing to look at, just desert, she was shocked. She admitted that at one point she wanted to go back home, and she was scared. I mean, I could not blame her. This was all new to us both. Look at us: I was nineteen years old and she was eighteen years old with a six-month-old baby, three thousand miles away from home with no family support. We were alone. As time went by, Vivian was starting to settle in and get used to the surroundings. She started to fall in love with the desert as I had. We always said when in retirement, we would be living in the southwest desert somewhere.

Around February or March 1990, we both found out Vivian was pregnant again! Anthony Jr. would become a big brother come October, when Vivian would be due. We were happy about that. Life went on for the three of us, soon to be four. All was going well. I still had a lot of training to do, so I would have to leave to the field for days on end for training exercises. I hated leaving Vivian and the baby alone. I would be gone from a couple of days to weeks at a time.

Vivian's older sister was getting married in August, so we were preparing for a cross-country drive back to Ohio for the wedding. We made it in thirty-six hours. We drove straight through. Not bad. We made it and attended Vivian's sister's August 4 wedding, which was a lot of fun. It was nice to be home with family and friends. We had missed them all.

We might have been home approximately four days or so when my first sergeant called from California. I was supposed to be on leave for about twenty days. My first sergeant stated, "You need to get back to California as soon as possible." I did not know at the time what was happening in the Persian Gulf. I was not watching any news or reading the newspaper. I had to tell him I had driven here with my family, and would I be able to drive back with them? He said, "No, you have to get on a plane and get back." I had to leave the car and my family there in Ohio and had to get on the next available flight back to California.

I flew out the next day, and when I got back, it was hectic. Everyone was packing their gear and weapons and getting ready to deploy overseas to Saudi Arabia. Every day, we would wonder if that would be the day we were going, but it would be a false alarm. It went on like that for about a week or so. Vivian eventually flew out a couple of days after I did. She had to be there with me and see me off when I left.

The day finally came about a week later. I think it was the fifteenth of August when we got the call. I got all my stuff together and said goodbye to Vivian and Anthony Jr. By this time, Vivian was six or seven months pregnant. We both cried saying goodbye to each other. I gave them both a big hug and kiss. My neighbor was taking me to drop me off at my unit. The last thing I saw was Anthony Jr. standing at the screen door watching me leave. That was tough, not to just lose it at that moment. I was able to keep it together and focus on what was coming next: *war!*

I was dropped off, and once again, it was chaos. Higher-ranking marines were barking orders on what we needed to take or leave behind. The buses finally arrived to take us to Norton Air Force Base. After we arrived at Norton AFB, they started to pass out all our ammunition, and that is when it hit me: *I am going to war, combat, and there is a chance I might not come back.* What a horrible feeling. We flew twenty-two total hours in a C141 cargo plane to Saudi Arabia, stopping in Naval Air Station Rota, Spain, and Germany on the way.

IRAQI INVASION OF KUWAIT

On August 2, 1990, the Iraqi army began the occupation of Kuwait. From August 2, 1990, to about January 17, 1991, began Operation Desert Shield, leading to the buildup of troops and defense of Saudi Arabia. Saudi Arabia thought the Iraqi army would continue south into their country and invade them as well. So, during this time, we were protecting the country of Saudi Arabia. The higher-ups—POTUS, generals—were in talks with Iraq to leave Kuwait for a little over four months. They gave Iraq (Saddam Hussein) plenty of opportunity to leave Kuwait.

On January 17, 1991, Operation Desert Storm began. That was the combat phase of the war. Now instead of playing defense and protecting Saudi Arabia from a potential invasion, it was decided to go on the offensive and get the Iraqi army out of Kuwait. We began to move north toward Kuwait. Little by little, we would get closer. The bombardment of the US and Coalition forces began. You could feel the ground shaking and trembling all day and all night. They were getting hammered up there. At nighttime, you could see all the flashes of the bombs exploding, and we were still miles away. The closer we got, the brighter and louder the flashes got and the harder the ground shook. (No wonder I hate Fourth of July.) Just constant bombing.

Even though I was in an AAV, I was attached to Third Tank Battalion, Bravo Command Element, Task Force Ripper as their communications vehicle. I had the commander of the

Bravo Command Element riding with me to include ten other officers who had constant contact with air, land, and sea. We were, as we called it, the tip of the spear. We were going to be in the middle of the shit when it all went down. I felt we were safe, being that we were surrounded by a battalion of tanks. So, we kept on heading north toward Kuwait. We ended up just a few miles from the Kuwaiti border. Let me tell you, the sound of those bombs being dropped onto the Iraqi army was scary. I was just glad I was on the good guys' team. How can anyone survive that?

(Just to back up the story a bit, October 19, 1990, Vivian gave birth to Justin, our second son. I was notified by a Red Cross message of the news. I was able to call home and talk to Vivian to make sure all was well with her and the baby. I missed her so much, and my kids.)

We were so close to the border that it felt like the bombs were falling on us. Especially when the B-52s dropped their load; it was like an earthquake was happening. Everyone was getting their last orders and packing up all loose gear in preparation for our assault into Kuwait. Nobody really talked to one another. We basically stayed to ourselves, and you could feel the nervousness everyone was feeling. We were about to go to war. *Fuck! This is for real! I could die and not get to see my family again. I may not get to see my new son!*

About 3:00 a.m. on February 24, 1991, we started our movement north toward Kuwait. Ahead of us were a battalion of tanks leading the way. Being a command element, we had to stay back a few hundred yards with our escorts close by. Our escorts consisted of fully armored Humvees loaded to the gills with weapons, such as .50 caliber machine guns and 40 mm grenade launchers. They were our protection. Slowly, but surely, we were getting closer to the border. Approximately an hour later, I heard over my helmet communications that we had just crossed into Kuwait. My adrenaline went through the roof! This was happening for real. It was still dark, and we barely could see anything. We kept on moving north slowly through Kuwait. I would say for an hour into Kuwait, we received no resistance. It was like nobody was out there.

Then at dawn, that all changed. We came up to our first minefield that the Iraqi army had placed. The battalion stopped prior to the minefield. Some Iraqi army were there and were firing mortar rockets in our direction. Then I saw one of our tanks shoot their tank round down range toward the resistance. It started; my war has begun. I began to cry and was screaming to "get those motherfuckers!" I did not feel fear; I was just happy that it had finally started. No more waiting. *Let us get this shit done and go home!*

Tank round after tank round were just going down range to where the enemy was at. What a sight to see. It was so awesome! That must have lasted an hour or so. What was left of the Iraqi soldiers there surrendered, I could not even tell you how many were killed. Once the minefield was cleared by our engineers, we continued north toward Kuwait City.

Approximately an hour later, we came upon a second minefield and encountered massive resistance. Once again, the tanks did their thing, just blowing shit up. Enemy mortar rockets again began to explode all around us. It seemed like hundreds of mortars were striking nearby. This was when the fear actually began to hit me. All I thought was, *Is the next mortar the one? Is the next mortar going to be the one that hits me and ends it all?* All I could think of was Vivian and the kids. I still had not seen my new baby.

This part of the battle lasted what seemed like forever. I was trying to drive this twenty-six-ton vehicle and zigzag to prevent getting hit by all the mortar rockets exploding all around us. At one point, I yelled out and pretty much gave up and said, "Hit me already! End it! What are you waiting for?" There were so many bombs falling around us that I do not know how we made it through that. Some were not lucky as we were. I could see a hundred yards in front of me, and enemy Iraqi fighters were just falling to the ground. I knew that they were getting killed. Iraqi vehicles, to include tanks, were getting blown to pieces. What a sight to see. I would not wish it on anyone. War is horrible. War will fuck you up. It is not normal. This shit is crazy!

After what seemed hours of battle, once again we had some Iraqi army surrender. Most were killed. The engineers cleared the second minefield, so we could continue north. It had been daylight for a while. Thank goodness it was. I could not imagine all this going on at dark hours. We continued north for a while and suddenly came upon a traffic control tower from which we were getting sniper fire. We could not move until the sniper was dealt with. At that time, a SuperCobra attack helicopter was called in, and within a few minutes of the Cobra being there, the tower was obliterated.

As we continued, we started seeing all the oil wells that had been purposely set on fire by the Iraqis. Had to have been dozens and dozens of wells on fire. The sky went dark from all the black sulfur smoke from the oil wells. It was midafternoon, and it seemed like it was nighttime. Here we were in the middle of this burning black sulfur, so thick you could barely see two feet in front of you. I am sure I will feel the effects of this later in life. We even settled in for the night in the middle of this stuff. It was awful breathing this stuff in.

The next day, we prepared to move north toward Kuwait City. It was morning, but again it looked like it was midnight. Those oil wells were burning pretty well. We finally got far enough from the wells that the sky began to clear up, and we saw the daylight. We came upon small firefights on our trek north, but I think the Iraqi army by this time was tired, hungry, and ready to give up. Most of them were ready to surrender by then.

The last obstacle we had to get through was an orchard

just outside the limits of Kuwait City. It looked like a big forest in the middle of the desert. We had to go through it to get to the city. We had intelligence that some Iraqi tanks and other weapons were in the orchard dug in, waiting for us. As we approached, our battalion of tanks led the way, with Cobra helicopters on standby. We encountered some resistance, but they were taken care of immediately by our tanks. We finally got through the orchard and could see the outskirts of Kuwait City. As we got closer, you could see all the damage to all the buildings from the bombings. Just an awful sight to see. We settled in just outside of the city awaiting orders. Unknown to us, as we were liberating the city, most of the Iraqi army was fleeing north back to Iraq. They tried to use a highway to flee north, which is now known as the "highway of hell" due to the US and Coalition air forces bombing this highway as they were fleeing, killing thousands.

The city was now safe to enter, and all the Kuwaitis who had stayed during this whole ordeal came running up to us, hugging and kissing us and thanking us for liberating them. It was a great feeling. Besides a few firefights up north closer to the Iraqi border, the war was pretty much over. It was a short war, a few days long, but a violent one, and I made it! I was going to see my family!

We stayed a couple of more days, and then we started to head south back to Saudi Arabia. As we were heading south, the people lined the sides of the roads and waved the American flag at us as we drove by and thanked us. It took us a day or two to get back to our actual base camp. From there, we waited maybe a couple of weeks, and we got our orders that we were going home. Man, that was a great feeling.

It was about the end of March 1991 when we finally left. Almost eight months deployed away from my family. There were moments I thought I would not come back, but there I was, finally about to go home. When the time came to go home, we boarded an air force C-5 Galaxy, a much more comfortable ride than we had had when we were coming. As soon as we got out of Saudi Arabian airspace, one of the crew members came out with cases of Budweiser and started passing them out to us. He was congratulating us on a job well done. It was my first beer in eight months, since no alcohol is allowed in Saudi Arabia. I think I drank two beers and passed out for the rest of the flight. We stopped in Germany for refuel. Then we were off again; this time, the next stop would be on US soil at Dover Air Force Base in Delaware.

Once we landed, they put us on a shuttle bus to take us to one of the hangers, where they had refreshments waiting for us. To my surprise, that was not all. I could not believe what I was seeing as we were pulling up. It was like we were going to the Academy Awards. Hundreds of people were waiting for us. They had a red carpet on the ground leading us into the hanger. All the clapping and cheering and gratitude these people had for us was amazing. I felt so proud at that moment.

I felt so proud to be a marine, and most of all, I felt so proud to be an American. We stayed there for a few hours and enjoyed the company of complete strangers who treated us like family. Plus, we finally were able to have our first decent meal in a long time.

Our stay was coming to an end, and we were to board again and head to our final stop, Norton AFB in California. I could not wait to get home. When we arrived on the West Coast, it was early in the morning. We got off the plane and onto two or three buses that were waiting for us to take us to base. There was where our families would be waiting for us. It was about a two-hour bus ride back to Twentynine Palms. I was getting anxious. I was about to see my family—and to see Justin, who had just been born six months ago, for the first time. Yeah, I was nervous.

After the long bus ride, I saw the front gate of the base: "Welcome to MCAGCC (Marine Corps Air Ground Combat Center) 29 Palms, CA." I was home, finally! The bus drove a little longer, and I could see a crowd of people up ahead waiting. We pulled up and stopped. I was scared to get off the bus. I did not know what to expect when I got to see Vivian and the kids. Once I got off the bus, I saw Vivian. She was holding Justin. Anthony Jr. was standing next to her. We all just walked up to one another and kissed and hugged one another tight. I took Justin from Vivian and was holding my six-month-old son; he just stared at me like, "Who are you?"

I thanked God and felt grateful that I was able to be there at that moment with my family again. Anthony Jr. had gotten so big! The last memory I had of him was when he was standing at the screen door looking out when I left. I was so glad that he was happy to see me and that he remembered me.

We got all our gear off the bus and went home. I remember at one-point Vivian and I were talking, and she stopped and was staring at me. I was thinking to myself; *Did I say something wrong?* She just looked at me and said that I had changed, and I was different. I told her I was fine, not knowing at the time how war can change a person.

Everything went back to normal at home and at work. We continued to train and hold field exercises, days or weeks at a time. My enlistment was coming to an end. We had to decide whether I was going to reenlist or get out. After I talked about it with Vivian, we decided to stay in for another four years. So, I went ahead and reenlisted and was going to be assigned as an instructor at the AAV school at Camp Pendleton, California. We were to leave the desert for the sunny beaches.

June 1992, we packed up a U-Haul and towed our car and headed one and a half hours southwest to Camp Pendleton, California, for my new duty assignment. This time, we decided not to live on base. We lived out in the city of Oceanside. We rented an apartment out there. It was kind of nice going to work and then actually leaving work (the base) and going home. It felt like a normal job.

It was a great assignment being an AAV instructor. Being that our job had to do with operations in the water, the school was located right by the beach. It was like going to the beach every day. My experience at Schools Battalion was great. It felt good passing on my knowledge to the new marines and having them graduate and sending them off to the FMF (Fleet Marine Force). It was very rewarding. During my career in the Marine Corps, I made it through the ranks respectfully, and while at Schools Battalion, I was promoted to the rank of sergeant.

September 1995, Vivian and I got to renew our vows in the same church her parents were married in. We always said we would get married by church one day. Also, that year was decision time once again as to whether I was going to reenlist for another four years or get out. If I stayed in, I wanted to be a drill instructor at one of the two boot camps. I also was taking police entry exams for neighboring cities so that just in case I did get out, I would have a job. Vivian and I talked about it once again, and the decision was made to get out and move back to Cleveland, Ohio, and be back with our family. February 1996, I would be honorably discharged from the United Stated Marine Corps.

CLEVELAND, OHIO

A FEW MONTHS WENT BY, AND I SAW THAT THE CITY OF Cleveland was preparing to start taking applications for patrol officers. I had a couple of friends who were police officers already, so I decided I would apply. After applying, I was given a test date. When I showed up to the written portion of the test, there had to be a couple of thousand applicants taking the test. Once the test was over, I waited about a month or so, and a letter came in the mail stating where I had finished on the list. I was 233 out of 1,500 or so. *Not bad,* I thought. As I was going through the hiring process, which took almost two years, I was employed with the local phone company as a communications technician.

I received the call to start the Cleveland Police 118th Academy class on September 28, 1998. The academy was about five months long. The first few weeks were spent taking care of administrative stuff. The academy was along the lines of a military atmosphere—which, of course, I would not have a problem with. For some, it was a culture shock, and we had a few dropouts due to the yelling and military-style teaching.

One day that I will remember and never forget was the day the department psychologist came in to talk to us. She stood up in front of the class of eighty recruits, looked at us, and stated, "Some of you are here because you want to do good and help people." Then she looked around and stated, "Some of you are here for the gun and the badge. You want to feel that power and be able to tell people what to do." Then she stated,

"But all of you sitting here today, and throughout your career as a police officer, will never be the same again." I sat there and wondered what she meant. That statement would become clearer and clearer to me as the years went by on this job.

The weeks went by quickly. We did a lot of training in class and out of class. Almost felt like I was back in the military again—almost. Graduation day was coming up fast, February 1999. It was on a Friday. The swear-in ceremony was nice. It was another proud day for me. The ceremony lasted for about an hour or so. We were now officially Cleveland police officers. They gave us the weekend off, and we were to report on Monday to our assigned district for work. I was assigned to the city's Second District, an area I grew up in since I was ten years old, when we moved from New York City. So, I was very familiar with the area. I would start my six-month probationary period and get assigned field training officers. For the next six months, I learned a lot from my FTOs. Got to see a whole lot of crazy stuff too. After my six months of probation were completed, I was a fully-fledged, certified officer. I could be on my own now without a partner.

I remember my first assignment after probation. I was a one-man car and was given a pedestrian struck by a vehicle. I pulled up to this scene, and it was complete chaos! All I thought was that I had to take charge of this scene and fast, but at the same time, I did not know what to do! I was so nervous! I basically got thrown into the fire. I called for a supervisor to respond on the scene, which he did. Thank God he was understanding and walked me through everything.

First couple of years of being on the job, I settled in nicely. I also got to handle and witness all types of crimes: assaults, child abuse, suicides, rapes, homicides, shootings—you name it, I saw it. I also got to understand that for every assignment you respond to and handle, you tend to take a little bit of it with you and keep it in and move on to the next. It takes a toll on you, not only physically, but mentally. You do not talk about it either. You learn from the veteran officers to suck it up. It is part of the job. You cannot show any sign of weakness. You know that *stigma*. After a while, Vivian was noticing a change in me. She would tell me to go and talk to someone. I always would tell her I felt fine. Must suck it up. It's part of the job.

We had a couple of officers from our district, whom I personally worked with, commit suicide. That was a rough time for all of us. Losing a brother in blue is a horrible experience, and we lost two, one day apart from each other. What did we do? We did what we usually did. We went back to work, and again, we kept it all in.

I continued to push through my career, going to work every day, still not talking about what I saw during my shifts. One summer, we had an officer shot and killed while conducting a traffic stop. Another year, we had another officer who was shot in the face with his own gun, after being tackled by a homeless man he had just finished giving a ride to. The officer survived. We had another officer shot and killed while serving an arrest warrant. But it's part of the job. *Suck it up, kid. Do not show any emotion. You're weak if you do. We will go to the bar after work and drink it all away.* That was the answer. My glass began to fill. I knew I was changing. Vivian obviously saw it, but I continued to refuse to talk to anyone. I was fine. I was a marine, I had been to war, and I could handle anything.

The trauma continued. Another officer was shot in the stomach investigating a bunch of young kids disturbing the neighborhood and drug activity. He died the next day. *When is this all going to end? My glass is filling pretty fast, and I do not know how long I can hold on.* Vivian continued to push for me to talk to someone. I knew she meant well. She cared for me, but I just could not do it. She began to tell me I was becoming short-tempered, always upset about small things. I would always yell at the kids, and at her too. As the years went by, I continued to push on. It was not all bad days at work. We did have good days. The bad ones just seem to stay with you.

More bad news: June 2011, my middle brother was diagnosed with stage 4 lung cancer. He was only forty-eight years old. That was tough on the family. We tried to be there for him and be as supportive as we could for him.

September 6, 2011, I reported to work. This was to be my day off, but they were short that day and they needed people, so I volunteered. I had a partner that day. The whole shift went smoothly, and we took our lunch around 8:00 p.m. Our lunch break was over, and it was almost 9:00 p.m. We both decided to go back out on patrol for a while before ending our shift at midnight. As we pulled out of the parking lot, my partner advised dispatch we were done with lunch.

Soon after that, dispatch advised us that she had a Code 1 for us. After my partner acknowledged her, she continued to state, "Multiple calls are coming in that someone was shot." After being given the address, we started heading over to that location. While we were en route to the location, dispatch was keeping us updated on the situation. At one point, dispatch stated, "I have a caller on the phone who states he just shot his girlfriend and that he will be waiting for the police when they get there." My partner and I just looked at each other with that *oh, shit!* look on our faces.

As I turned onto the street, it seemed like the whole block was out screaming at us, "He's over there!" For safety reasons, I was not going to rush up to the house in question. It was dark out, and I had the spotlight on trying to find the location of the residence. I was going about five to ten miles per hour down the street. I did not want to get ambushed if this guy still had the gun. I observed a house off to the right with the porch light on and a male and a female standing on the porch. I stopped the car about two or three houses prior to that house, and we got out of the car.

As we were walking up cautiously, the male jumped off

the porch with a gun in his hand and started yelling, "You all are going to have to kill me today!" I immediately raised my weapon and was yelling at him to drop his gun. He was refusing and began to walk backward. Now he had the gun pointed to his head, still yelling, "You all are going to have to kill me today!" Suicide by cop situation. The same time this was going on, the lady on the porch, who was the mother of the victim who was shot, was yelling at us to help her daughter inside the house. It was chaos! But my concentration was on the guy with the gun. I continued to give him orders to drop the gun, but he continued to refuse.

Other officers began to arrive to assist. EMS personnel could not get close enough to help the victim because the scene was not secured. Repeatedly, we pleaded with the male to drop the gun, but he continued to refuse our commands and always had the gun pointed to his head. He continued to state, "You all are going to have to kill me today!" By this time, he was standing in the middle of the street, and my tunnel vision began to kick in. I was focused on this guy and his gun. Then in an instant, he took the gun away from his head and pointed it at us. I fired two shots. Other officers on scene also fired their weapons. The male immediately went down to the ground. We cautiously walked up to the male, and he was lying there bleeding from his lower extremities. He was still alive. He wanted us to kill him, suicide by cop.

After we secured the scene, EMS was able to come onto the

scene and assist the victim who had been shot in the house. Another EMS wagon arrived for the male whom we had just shot. I was in a daze. I could not believe what had just happened. First chance I got, I called Vivian to let her know what had just happened and that I was OK. I became a little emotional about it. The emotions caught me off guard. *I am a marine, a combat veteran. Why is this bothering me? Maybe because it was more up close and personal? I do not know, but what I do know is I survived, and I will be going home tonight.* The female victim also survived her gunshot wound. The bullet just missed a major artery. The male suspect also survived his wounds. All officers who were involved in the shooting incident were placed on administrative leave, with transitional duty for about three months, prior to returning to full duty.

This was my chance to talk to someone about all the shit I was holding in. We needed to get cleared by a psychiatrist prior to returning, so this was it. Meanwhile, we had no psychologist on staff to talk to in the three months I was off. I had all this garbage I was holding in, and now I had a shooting on top of it and no one to talk to.

While I was off for the shooting, my middle brother's cancer was getting worse. He was in and out of the hospital and pretty much on bed rest. We all knew it was getting close to the end. They let him go home on hospice care. I tried to spend as much time as I could with him at his house while he was at home. My middle brother passed away November 2011. He was forty-eight years old. I miss him so much.

My three months were coming to an end, and I was ready to go back to work. Guess what I had to do before I got the OK to go back to work? The department decided to schedule me to see a psychiatrist. *Are you kidding me? What happened to the last three months?* So, I went in, and it lasted fifteen minutes, if that. Done. Cleared to go back to work. By now I had about thirteen years on the job. I decided to work a single response car, or one-man car. All by myself, I would only be responsible for handling minor crime reports or property damage reports. Nothing major. You can work at your own pace. I needed the break.

SUMMER 2012

VIVIAN'S YOUNGEST SISTER WAS ON THE JOB ALSO. SHE GOT on about two years after I did, so she had over ten years on. Her husband was also on the job. He got on much later and had about four or five years on. I was at work one night when I got a call from Vivian. She stated something had happened over at her sister's house, that she was on her way over there, and that I should go also. All I could think about was that her sister was eight months pregnant and something was wrong. I was able to leave work early and head to my sister-in-law's and brother-in-law's house. As I was pulling up, I can see there were police and EMS there in the driveway. I was confused. *What happened here?*

I parked my car, and as I was walking up the driveway, Vivian told me that my brother-in-law had shot himself and committed suicide. I was in shock! I had not known he was struggling in any way. No one had. *Oh my God, my sister-in-law! Eight months pregnant, and the baby will never know its father.* My brother-in-law was buried that Saturday with full department honors. Just two days later, on Monday, my sister-in-law gave birth to their son. If only he had gotten help or talked to someone, he could be alive today enjoying his son. *Maybe I need to follow this advice.* I took some days off after that to decompress. Just another trauma in my life I had to deal with. Just like I always did, I held it in and continued to push on with work and life. We helped my sister-in-law as much as we could. The whole family did. She was alone, a single mother, raising two kids. She was strong and handled it better than most would have. I was proud of her.

The rest of 2012 came and went. Work was work. Nothing new going on. Just the same old crimes being committed. It was nonstop. Again, I was a one-man car mostly, taking minor crime reports for the citizens. Around February or March 2013, I made the decision to get assigned back to a two-man car and have a partner again. I was trying to change it up and not get burnt out. I got assigned to 2A23 with a great guy, Officer Mike Tracy, He was about a year senior to me, but we had the same work ethics. Everything was going great working with my partner. It was a good change of pace. Home life I would say was fine, but I know Vivian would say different. She still wanted me to talk to someone and work out whatever she was seeing. Of course, it would be the "No, I am fine" response I would give her. I would continue to push on with work, not knowing that what would come next would change my life forever.

MAY 6, 2013

THE RESCUE

WE MADE OUR WAY TO SEYMOUR AVENUE, GETTING THERE within one minute of receiving the call. We saw a crowd that was gathered up ahead. I looked at Mike and kept asking him, "Is it her?", but we were not close enough yet. After getting close enough to the crowd, I could see a female holding a child walking up toward the driver's side. So, I asked Mike one last time, "Is it her?"

Mike turned and looked at me and said, "It's her." I felt like I had just gotten hit by a truck. After calling our arrival, I got out of the car and walked around the front of the car to where she was standing. I stood there looking at her, and inside, I was like, *Oh shit, it is Amanda Berry!* You could tell it was her. She was thinner and paler than her picture on the posters that were up all over the neighborhood. The one thing that stood out the most about her was the eyebrow ring that she had in, which you saw in all the pictures.

I still needed confirmation, so I asked for her name. She looked at me and stated, "I am Amanda Berry. I was kidnapped for ten years." Then she began to mention an Ariel Castro, who was the one who had taken her. As she was giving us all this information, I was broadcasting it over the radio. I also requested for a supervisor to respond to the scene. She kept on pointing to this house across the street, 2207 Seymour Avenue.

By this time, other officers were starting to arrive on scene. My partner, Mike, asked her, "Is there anyone else in the house?"

Amanda stated, "Gina DeJesus and another girl!" I looked at Mike and could not believe what she had just said! Gina DeJesus—just like Amanda, everyone knew who she was, and like Amanda, she had posters all over Cleveland.

Mike and I began to run toward 2207 Seymour Avenue. Other officers were on scene with Amanda. She was safe. All I could think of was Gina and this other girl still being in this house, and possibly this Ariel Castro as well. We got onto the porch and tried to open the screen door, but it would not open. It was held shut by a chain that was welded to the screen door and the doorjamb. My partner Mike decided to crawl through the bottom opening of the screen door that Amanda had kicked out and crawled through in which she was able to escape. Once Mike was inside, he began to kick the door from the inside to try and break the chain. Another officer crawled through the same opening and began to kick the door also. The chain finally broke, and the screen door opened.

We all rushed into the house. Mike and a few other officers started clearing the first floor. I immediately saw stairs to my right but could not access them because there was an outdoor swing set blocking the stairwell. I grabbed part of the swing set and moved it enough that I could access the stairs to go up. I began to climb the stairs very cautiously. I had my gun out at the ready position. I felt someone tap my gun belt from behind and say, "I got your back." It was Officer Barbara

Johnson, an outstanding police officer. I knew I was in good hands if anything went down.

We both continued to climb the stairs. I began to shout out, "Cleveland Police! Cleveland Police!" Everything was quiet. I was focused on a curtain covering the opening of the landing to the second floor. What was on the other side of the curtain? Was Ariel Castro standing there with a weapon, ready to take me out as soon as I pulled the curtain aside? That unknown feeling sucked. We reached the top of the landing, and I was ready. I reached out and pulled the curtain aside, and no one was there. It was dark and silent. I continued to call out, "Cleveland Police! Cleveland Police!" Nothing. It was so quiet, as if nobody were up here. I thought we would just clear the second floor and be done. There were a lot of kids' toys in the hall area. I saw a room to my left with a light on, and I could see a mattress on the floor. Everything was still quiet.

I called out a couple more times with my gun at the ready, "Cleveland Police! Cleveland Police!" That was when I heard some movement coming from that room to the left. Barb and I just froze, but we were ready for anything. Then I saw what I thought at the time was a small child peek around the door-jamb of the bedroom. She stood there staring at me as I was staring at her. It was like we were in a standoff of sorts. After a few moments, I said, "Cleveland Police," and at that moment, this person—this child, as I thought at the time—came charging at me, running at full speed.

I had no time to react, and she jumped on me, wrapping her arms around my neck, wrapping her legs around my waist. She began to yell, "You saved us! You saved us! My name is Michelle Knight. I am thirty-one years old, and I have been here for eleven years, and you saved us!" I thought I was holding a small child. Thirty-one years old? That is how tiny Michelle was. I had no words. I held on to her as tightly as I could.

Then I saw another person coming out of the same bedroom area. I put Michelle down, and she jumped into Barb's arms. As I looked up toward the doorway, I immediately knew who it was. I slowly walked toward her, and for confirmation, I asked her what her name was. She replied, "My name is Georgina DeJesus."

I had to hold it together. My emotions by this point were becoming uncontrollable. I could not believe what I was witnessing. It was so overwhelming. Now I had to broadcast over the radio who we had found upstairs. I took a few seconds to compose myself. If I had broadcasted right away, I would have broken down crying. Once I was ready, I grabbed my mic and stated, "2 Adam 23 to radio."

Dispatch responded, "2A23, go ahead."

Then that is when I broadcasted to dispatch, to the city, to the world, *We found them! We found them!*

After the broadcast, I knew we had to get both Michelle and Gina out of that house. I had to continue to try to keep my composure and stay focused. We asked the girls to grab what they could and to follow us out the house. They both ran back into the room off to the left, where they had come out of, and grabbed what they could. Michelle grabbed some clothes, but what stood out to me was what Gina grabbed. When Gina had been taken around nine years earlier, she was taken after school. She went back into that room and grabbed her book-bag she had from that day.

During this time, it was discovered that Ariel Castro was not in the house, and this information was passed on to dispatch and the other officers who were listening. Officers who were outside with Amanda were gathering more information on Ariel Castro. It was found out that he drove a Mazda Miata. Once the license plate was broadcasted by our dispatch, some officers broke away from the scene to search for this vehicle and suspect.

Meanwhile, Michelle and Gina were finishing up getting their belongings. While they were doing that, I just stood there looking around. What I saw was horrific. Padlocks on the doors, holes drilled into the doors big enough for him to pass food through to them while they were locked up. Heavy-duty chains that he would restrain them with. It was an unbelievable sight. I had to snap out of it, wherever I was, and get back to getting these girls out of here.

We finally got them out of there and walked them out to where an ambulance was waiting. Amanda was already in the ambulance with her child. The child she had been holding earlier when we first pulled up was her child. At that time, we did not know how this child fit in the scenario; now we know. The ambulance immediately left the area with Officer Barbara Johnson, heading for a nearby hospital. I was told that myself and other officers went back into the house to completely clear it and secure it, and till this day, I do not recall doing that.

I remember a detective coming up to me and asking me, "How were you able to concentrate with all that loud music playing in the house?"

I just looked at him dumbfounded and just said, "What music?" I did not hear anything.

He continued, "In the living room, there was a stereo playing full blast music the whole time we were in the house." I came to find out later that I had what was called auditory exclusion, which is a temporary loss of hearing occurring under stressful situations. Your senses shift, and you use what senses are more important at the time of the event. Never knew that.

The house was cleared, and we all got out and a few officers posted themselves at all the entrances, front and back, so the scene would not be compromised. While on scene, I began to tape off a large area to keep the crowd that was forming from entering the crime scene area. Word was traveling fast that the girls were found. Even the media was arriving. I heard over the radio that Ariel Castro's vehicle had been spotted at a fast-food restaurant not too far from our location. He was stopped and taken into custody with his brother, who later we found out after the investigation had nothing to do with the kidnappings. It was all Ariel. He kept this secret from his family and friends for approximately eleven years.

Commanders started to show up. The FBI was also on scene working the crime scene. County prosecutors were showing up also, asking me questions on what I had seen in the house in order to get all the necessary warrants. I do not know how many times that night I told the story of the rescue. Everything was so overwhelming and very emotional, but I had to keep it together. All the top brass was on scene here. *Cannot show any emotions. Suck it up, at least for now.*

We were on scene for around four to five hours, and then we were able to leave and go back to the district to do the reports and paperwork. It was still unbelievable what had just happened. The chances of finding one missing person alive after so many years is slim to none. We had found three that day! We got back to the district, and all the officers that were there were asking questions. So once again, I had to go through the whole story again. I think this time I could not hold back my emotions. My emotions came out a little, and I got a few hugs from fellow officers, and they complimented me on a job well done.

After that, I went into the report room and completed the reports required for the girls being found. Michelle's initial missing person report had been filed in 2002. Amanda's had been filed in 2003, and Gina's in 2004. It was an honor completing each of these reports and stating that these girls had been found safe and alive. Officer Barbara Johnson had returned from the hospital and had to complete a report herself. We left to go home around midnight, and I felt bad that Barb did not get to go home until 3:00 or 4:00 a.m. It was a tough day for all of us.

Once I got home, Vivian was still up waiting for me. She could not wait to hear everything that had happened. When I was telling her, she just sat there in awe. She even got emotional at some point in the story. She was proud that I was one of the officers there.

The next week or so was very hectic. Our PIO (public information officer) kept getting calls that certain media entities wanted to sit down with us and interview us on what had happened in the house. At that time, we could not release any information on the case because it was still an active investigation. I had a major news agency knocking at my door at home wanting an interview. Luckily, Vivian answered the door both times. I was not used to the attention. I am a quiet, behind-the-scenes type of guy, and then suddenly, I was part of worldwide news. I was getting calls from family and friends saying that they had seen me on TV and they were showing my picture all over the news. We did end up doing a few interviews with our local news and did one with a major news outlet. We kept on getting requests to do more interviews, but we began to turn them down. It was getting too much for me to handle at the time. During the investigation and trial of Ariel Castro, he was found guilty on numerous counts of kidnapping, rape, and murder. He was sentenced to life plus a thousand years in prison. Unfortunately, he did not even serve a month in prison for his crimes. He ended up committing suicide.

THE AFTERMATH

AFTER A WHILE, I FELL INTO A FUNK. I COULD NOT EXPLAIN why I was feeling this way. Every time someone would bring up the rescue on Seymour, I would get upset. I did not know why. Such a positive moment for everyone, but I did not feel good about it.

Then suddenly, I started getting this memory from when I was six years old. I did not know why I was thinking about this memory or flashbacks, but they would not go away. I had to call my mom and ask her if the memories or flashbacks I was having were true. My mother stayed quiet for a few seconds and then asked why I was asking about that. I told her I had been getting these memories for a while of this incident and wanted to know if it was true. My mother confirmed that the memories and flashbacks that I was having were real and true. So, at the age of six years old, while living in Queens, New York, I was a kidnap victim myself. I guess it was suppressed all these years and the rescue on Seymour had triggered the memory. This is a memory that was buried for thirty-seven years!

In 1976, I was with my best friend sitting on the front stairs of my apartment building when two young women walked up to us asking for directions. My best friend, who was older than I was, was going to show them where to go, but they insisted that I show them the way. So, I agreed and got up and started walking them toward the area they were asking about. They were probably both in their late teens or early twenties. Once we got far enough from my apartment building, one of them grabbed my arm and would not let go. I was like, "What are you doing?" She held me tight and was pulling me toward a different direction. I began to cry and ask, "Where are you taking me?"

She responded, "We are taking you to the river to drown you and kill you!" I lived close to the East River at the time. I was terrified, and I thought I was going to die. I could not stop crying, and I was pleading with them to let me go. All they kept saying was that they were going to kill me. It felt like an eternity as we were walking. Right before we got to the river, which was by park access, the one who had me by the arm just looked at me and asked, "If we let you go, you promise not to tell anyone?"

I immediately agreed. She then let me go. I do not think I ever ran so fast in my life as I did to get away from them and to get back home. As I got closer to home, I could see my mom standing in front of the building looking for me. My best friend must have told her I had left with these two girls. I ran into my mother's arms like Michelle ran into mine in the house on Seymour. I told her everything. I must have been gone for about thirty to forty-five minutes. Back then, there was no calling the police. The family took care of any problems. For the next few days, my family searched for these girls, but they were never found.

So that is why I was such in a funk and not feeling right

about the rescue. It bothered me because I could relate. I continued to struggle. I kept on replaying the rescue and, of course, my kidnapping at age six. I just could not get it out of my mind. I believe that was the point where I started to become overwhelmed and tired. Not the kind of tired that meant I needed sleep either. My glass was overflowing now.

I started to isolate myself from everyone. I would not go to any family functions or hang out with my friends. It was getting worse and worse. Everything was catching up to me at once. From combat to my shooting to all the accumulated stress from the job to my fellow officers committing suicide, and my brother-in-law doing the same, to the rescue on Seymour—man, that screwed me up. That was personal. I needed the pain to go away. I was tired. I did not want to do this anymore. Vivian had always told me to go see someone. Was this why? Was this what she was seeing?

Vivian would get off work at 5:00 p.m. but would never come straight home. When she did, she would always call first to see if I picked up the phone. One day, I asked her why she did that, and she said she was afraid that one day she would come home and find me. I had never thought it would get this far, but I was at a breaking point. All I saw were two options: make the phone call and ask for help or take my gun and end the pain.

Nobody was home on September 14, 2015. Vivian was at work, and I was just waking up from working the night shift.

Nothing special about this day, but it would be the day I would make my decision. I had the phone in one hand and my gun in the other. *How did I get here?* I felt so alone and scared. I did not know what to do. I was such in a dark place. *Will my family be OK when I am gone? I am so tired, really tired. I do not want to be here anymore. What am I going to do?* I sat in my room for a while thinking on what option I was going to take. I was so lost. *God, please help me. I know I have not talked to you in a while, but I really do not want to die. I do not want Vivian to come home and find me.*

Suddenly, I realized that I was dialing the phone. I knew God was with me that day because that phone had to have weighed about a thousand pounds, and for me to pick that phone up and start dialing, God had to have helped me. It would have been easier to pull the trigger. I was calling our employee assistance unit (EAU). I put my gun down and waited for someone to pick up the call. A detective picked up the phone and walked me through the process I had to go through, and he kind of talked me down. After that, I called Vivian at work to let her know that I had called for the help she had always wanted me to get all these years.

When she got home from work that day, I could see how grateful she was that I had made the call. It was like a big weight fell off the both of us. I ended up taking a couple of sick days off work and made an appointment to see the department psychologist. At my appointment, I was immediately diagnosed with accumulative posttraumatic stress disorder (PTSD). I went home and told Vivian, and we both cried.

I was reassigned from the Cleveland Police Second District to the Cleveland Police Headquarters, located in downtown Cleveland. I was on desk duty from here on out. I also got to see a psychiatrist, who confirmed the PTSD diagnosis and also diagnosed me with major depression and general anxiety. My life would never be the same again. Sound familiar? Academy class, seventeen years earlier, the statement the department's psychologist made. Now I realized what she had meant by that statement.

ROAD TO RECOVERY

IT TOOK ME A WHILE TO ACCEPT THE DIAGNOSIS THE DOCTORS gave me. I was embarrassed and kept it to myself. There is no way anyone in this profession would work with someone diagnosed with PTSD, major depression, and anxiety and on medication. That is the stigma we grew up with on this job. I entered a partial hospitalization program (PHP). I decided I was not going to sit on my ass and feel sorry for myself. I started doing research and educating myself on what I had and was going to classes and getting certifications to help other officers and veterans who were suffering as I was. I became a peer support officer for the department and became a very vocal advocate for mental health for all officers within the division. By this time, I did not give a shit who knew what I had and what I was going through. I was more focused on helping others.

Now, do not get me wrong, I do still have my bad days. There are days that I do not feel relevant. Why am I here? Then I think back on all the good I have done throughout my life by helping others and I realize, *You know what? I did make something of myself. I am relevant.*

I started evidence-based treatments for PTSD, individually and in group settings. Also, presently I am working with a psychologist. I began to travel on occasion with an organization that travels the country and teaches updated law enforcement tactics and procedures. I get to speak on the emotional aspects of the job and awareness. This is all therapy for me. The more

I share my story, the more I tend to heal and as I share my story, people from around the country hear about it and ask if I can speak at one of their seminars. It is very humbling when people want to hear about you.

So, I look back on life and say I lived a life full of major events, both good and bad. I am also here to say I am relevant. I believe that God has a purpose for me and that I am doing his work in helping others. As far as retirement, I was able to retire with a full pension with a total of twenty-five years of service. Vivian and I were able to do what we wanted to do when we retired. We relocated from Cleveland, Ohio, to the southwest deserts of the United States, to the Las Vegas area, and are enjoying every minute of it.

As for Amanda, Gina, and Michelle (Lily Rose), they are doing well and are living their lives to the fullest.

ABOUT THE AUTHOR

Anthony Espada is an eight-year Marine Corps Combat Veteran who retired from the Cleveland Police Department in Ohio after twenty-five years of service. During his police service, he was one of the primary officers involved in the rescue of three missing young women in Cleveland on May 6, 2013, which became a worldwide news event.

CPSIA information can be obtained
at www.ICGtesting.com
Printed in the USA
BVHW030838060221
599516BV00008BA/125

9 781665 701495